T5-AFT-364

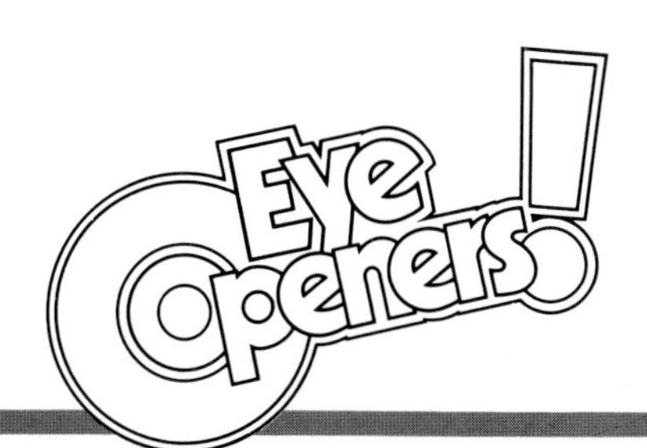

ANIMAL RECORD BREAKERS

SU SWALLOW

MACDONALD

Editor Susan Simpson
Designer Richard Garratt
Art Director Peter Luff

Illustrated by:
Fred Anderson
Richard Hook
Eric Jewell & Associates
David Kerr
Temple Art Agency
Chris Warner
Mike Welply

Published for Kmart Corporation
Troy, Michigan 48084

Conceived and produced by
Theorem Publishing Limited
71-3 Great Portland Street
London W1N 5DH

First published in 1981 by
Macdonald Educational Ltd.
Holywell House
Worship Street
London EC2A 2EN

ISBN 0 356 07093 X

Printed in Hong Kong

Key to cover

1. There is a very good reason why the blue whale, the largest animal in the world, lives in the sea and not on land. Turn to page 4 for the answer.

2. This is the characteristic pose of a cobra when warding off an attacker. You can read more about animal defence on pages 10 and 11 and pages 26-30.

3. The smallest bird in the world is Helena's hummingbird. Yet it has a big appetite. Why? See page 7.

4. Pufferfish is a very good name for this kind of fish. To find out why, turn to page 11.

5. If cheetahs are the fastest animals in the world, why do they not always catch their prey? See page 22.

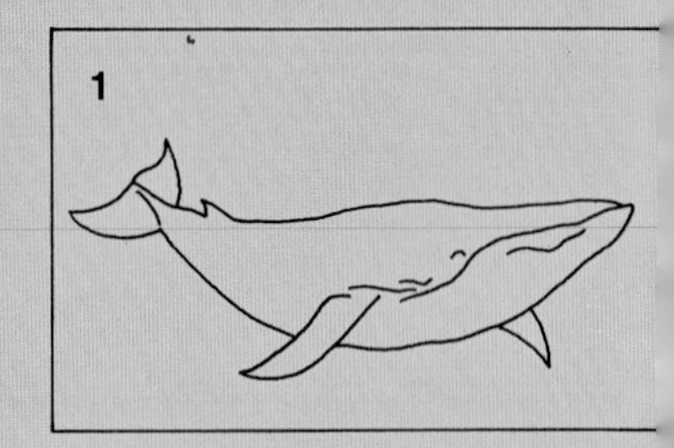

ANIMAL RECORD BREAKERS

The world is full of the most astonishing variety of animals. In size alone, the range is enormous. Among the mammals, a blue whale may reach 100 feet or more, while a rare kind of bat measures just 6 inches from wingtip to wingtip. Read about the animal athletes, the cheetah that can outpace a motor-car or the puma that can long jump twice as far as any human. Find out about the extraordinary use of camouflage and how some animals can tackle prey much larger than themselves. Turn to the back of the book for a quick reference guide to the record-breaking animals of the world.

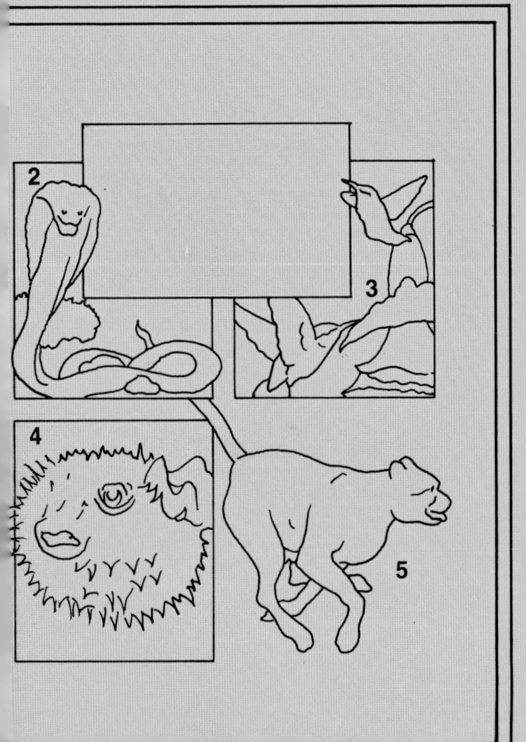

CONTENTS

Animal Giants

The animal giant of all time, the blue whale, is about 30 times heavier than the largest land animal. It is not by chance that this record-breaker should live in the sea. No land animal could ever reach that size because its weight would crush its bones. The whale's massive bulk, on the other hand, is supported by the water. The size of insects is limited for another reason. Insects have no lungs. Instead, most of them take in air through holes in the sides of their body. The oxygen is carried round the body by tubes. This system of breathing does not work very well above a certain size, so even the biggest insects are only as big as the smallest mammals.

All neck and legs
The giraffe, the tallest animal in the world, lives on the African plains. It can reach high into the trees, especially acacias, to feed, and can run at nearly 30 mph.

Huge but harmless
The rare blue whale, which can live for up to 100 years, is the largest and heaviest animal in the world. A fully grown blue whale may be 100 feet long, much bigger and heavier than any dinosaur that ever lived. Even a new-born blue whale is bigger than an adult elephant. Yet this monster mammal only eats tiny shrimp-like animals, called krill.

Killer crocodile
Crocodiles are the largest reptiles, and the estuarine crocodile, at nearly 30 feet, is the largest of them all. It is also one of the most dangerous, since it often adds people to its diet of fish and animals.

Great glider
The wandering albatross has the largest wing span of any bird, about as wide as two adults' outstretched arms. Its long thin wings allow it to glide for hours over the sea.

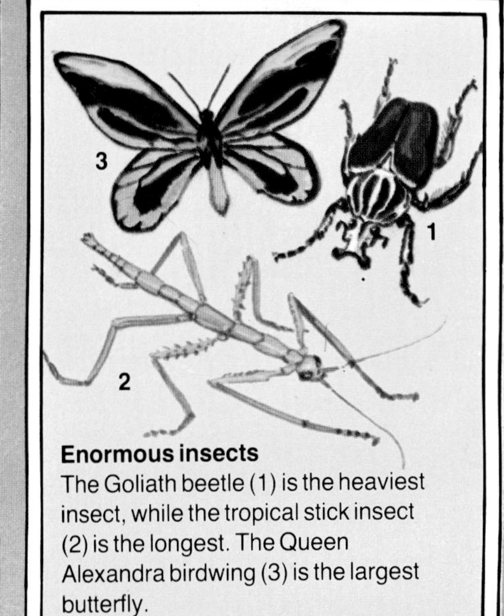

Enormous insects
The Goliath beetle (1) is the heaviest insect, while the tropical stick insect (2) is the longest. The Queen Alexandra birdwing (3) is the largest butterfly.

Largest on the land
The massive size and strength of the African elephant, the largest land animal, has not saved it from the hunter's gun. Elephants are now protected in the African game parks.

Seashore surprise
The longest animal in the world lives on the seashore. The bootlace ribbon worm, between 15 and 245 feet long, lives in an untidy coil under stones. It has lots of eyes.

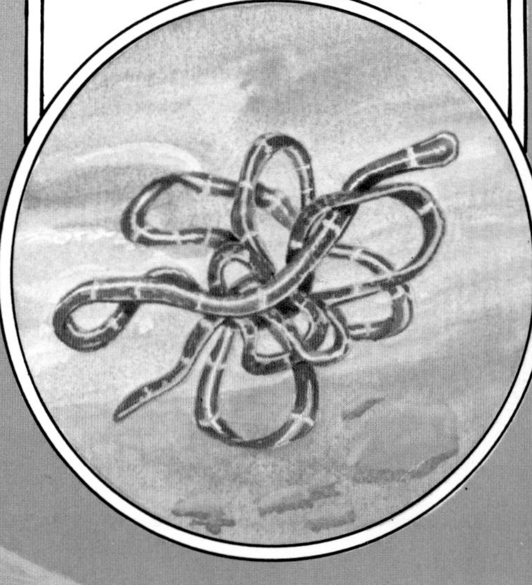

Mammal midget
These rare bats, called Kitti's hog-nosed bats, live in two caves near a river in Thailand. They are also called bumblebee bats because they are so small. In fact, they are the smallest of all mammals. Bats are the only mammals that fly.

Always hungry
Shrews belong to a group of insect-eating mammals called insectivores. Although shrews are so small, they need to feed almost constantly. They use their long snout to burrow among leaves and undergrowth in search of insects, worms and other small animals. Savi's white-toothed pygmy shrew, with a body only 1½ or 2 inches long, is the smallest insectivore. Here, it is drawn to the same scale as the ladybird.

Streamlined swimmer
Heaviside's dolphin is only a few feet long and is probably the smallest mammal in the sea. A dolphin's streamlined shape helps it to reach speeds of up to 25 mph as it chases after fish and squid. It can jump right out of the water.

Animals in Miniature

All these animals hold records for being the smallest of their kind. One, the hummingbird, holds several records. It is not only the smallest bird in the world, it also lays the smallest eggs (although they are large compared with the size of the bird). Its wing-beat is also the fastest of any bird. This feat uses up a lot of energy, so the hummingbird has to eat twice its weight in food every day. Some of these animals are rarer than their larger relatives. Indeed, the tiny bumblebee bat is only found in one place in the world. No-one knew about it until it was discovered in two caves in Thailand a few years ago.

A bird that hums
Helena's hummingbird, which lives in Cuba, is the smallest bird in the world. Its wings make a bee-like hum as they beat at 100 times a second. Hummingbirds hover to feed and can even fly backwards.

Shy forest-dwellers
These royal antelopes live in the thick forests of West Africa. They are the smallest of the antelopes, only 10 or 11 inches high at the shoulder (about the height of this book). They are agile, alert animals, and will dart into the undergrowth at the slightest sound or smell of danger.

Claws for climbing
The pygmy marmoset, whose body is only 4 inches long, lives in the forests along the Amazon river, in South America. It is the smallest monkey in the world. Unlike other monkeys, marmosets have claws for gripping on to the bark as they climb trees. They curl their long tail round branches to help them balance. They eat insects and nuts.

A fish out of water
The lungfish lives in tropical rivers. If its river dries up it makes a cocoon in the mud, with a hole up to the surface to let in air. It has lungs for breathing.

Monkey tricks
In Japan, where these macaque monkeys live, the winters are very cold. The Japanese macaques have shaggy coats to keep them warm, and some keep out the cold by sitting in the hot water from volcanic springs.

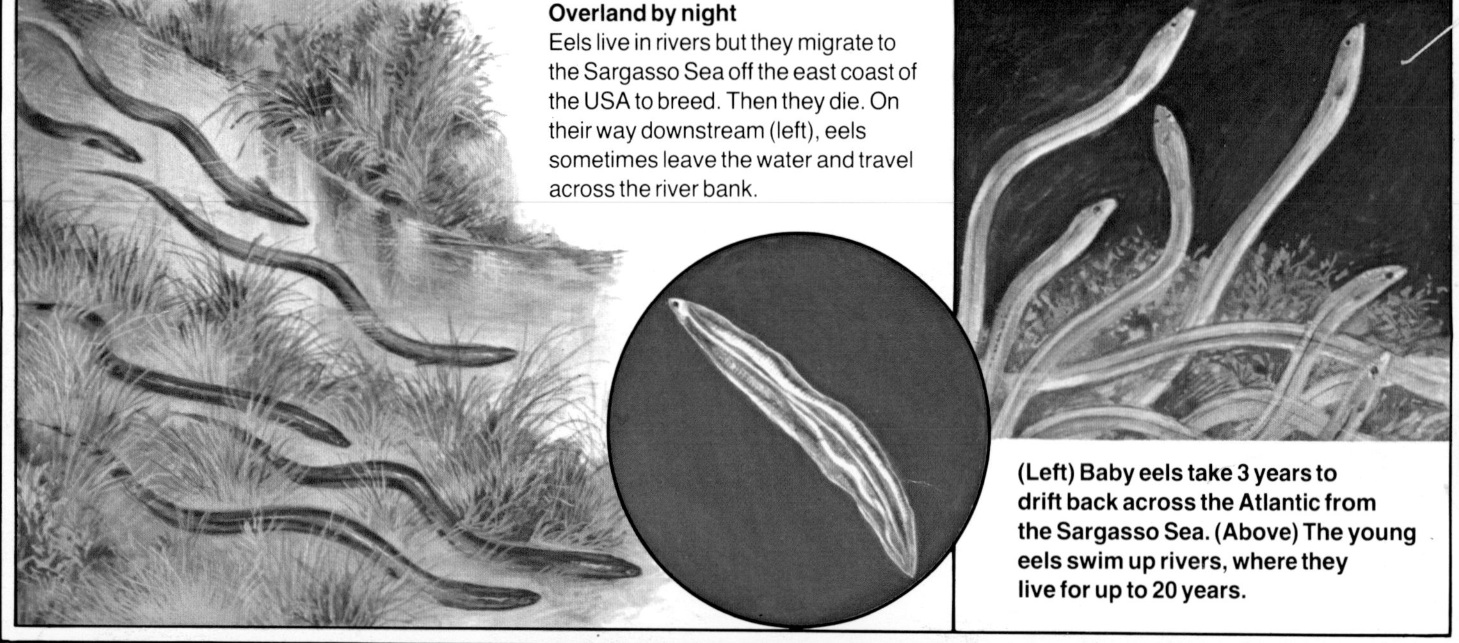

Overland by night
Eels live in rivers but they migrate to the Sargasso Sea off the east coast of the USA to breed. Then they die. On their way downstream (left), eels sometimes leave the water and travel across the river bank.

(Left) Baby eels take 3 years to drift back across the Atlantic from the Sargasso Sea. (Above) The young eels swim up rivers, where they live for up to 20 years.

Strange Haunts

Nature is full of surprises. Some of the animals shown here live in places where you would not expect to find them. Others have found unusual ways to make use of their strange surroundings. The vast majority of fish, for example, live in water and breathe with gills, yet one fish has developed lungs so that it can live in dried-up mud. Frogs, too, do not usually live far from water. Yet one kind can survive long periods of drought in the Australian desert. Such extreme examples of animal adaptation show how life can survive in even the most hostile environment. In fact, there are very few places on Earth that do not contain *some* form of life.

Amazing survival
This water-holding frog lives in the desert. When it rains, the frog absorbs water through its skin. Then it burrows into the sand, where it can stay for over two years until the next rainfall.

A hot spot
Most birds sit on their eggs to incubate them, but not this common scrub hen. Instead, it uses the heat from volcanoes to keep its eggs warm. It buries its eggs in the side of a volcano on the Pacific island where it lives.

Flying high
Bumble bees live high up in the mountains in Europe, where they feed on the pollen and nectar of the flowers that grow there. Some insects even fly over the snowy peaks of the Himalayas as they migrate.

Surprise tactics
The fire-bellied toad turns on its back when it is alarmed to display its bright belly. This sudden show of colour is often enough to startle its enemy. It is also a warning that the toad's skin is poisonous.

Owl alert
This is how the long-eared owl faces the enemy. When danger threatens, it makes itself look as large and fierce as possible, by fluffing out its feathers, spreading its wings and opening its eyes wide.

Smoke screen
A frightened squid squirts a kind of ink into the water. The ink spreads out like a black cloud and hides the squid. Then the squid can escape. Some deep-sea squids make a luminous cloud to dazzle the enemy.

Red in the face
When the puss moth caterpillar is disturbed, it lifts up its red face, and two long red 'whips' flick out of its tail. It also produces a smelly fluid, which it can even spray at its attacker.

A prickly mouthful
Pufferfish can fill themselves up with water so that they are too big to swallow. The porcupine fish has spines which stick out when it blows itself up. Its warning colours show up more clearly then, too.

Facing the Enemy

When an animal comes face to face with an enemy and cannot escape, it may still be able to protect itself in other ways. Some animals can trick their attacker into thinking they are more dangerous than they really are. They often do this by making themselves look very big and fierce. Colour is an important part of defence in the animal kingdom. It is often used for camouflage. Some animals have bright warning colours, especially red, yellow and black, which warn the enemy that they are poisonous and should be left alone. Other animals, though harmless, may use the same colours to fool their predators.

Dead or alive?
Some snakes, like this grass snake, escape capture by pretending to be dead already. Most meat-eating animals only feed on freshly-killed prey, and avoid animals that may have been dead for some time.

All eyes
This Indian cobra is trying to frighten away its attacker, the mongoose. The cobra rears up and spreads its hood. This stretches the skin of the hood so much that the eye markings show through to the front.

Threatening display
The Australian frilled lizard can frighten off an intruder by suddenly spreading out its huge neck frill. It opens its mouth wide, too, to look more fierce.

Bright bait
Clownfish are safe as long as they swim among the stinging tentacles of the giant sea anemone. Any fish that tries to catch them may end up as a meal for the sea anemone instead. The clownfish are covered in a sticky mucus that stops them being stung by the sea anemone.

Sharing a bees' nest
This bird, the greater honeyguide, leads the ratel, or honey badger, to a bees' nest by calling out and flying in front of it. The ratel eats the honey, then the bird eats the honeycomb wax.

Sentry duty
Red-billed ox-peckers keep a look-out for danger in return for food. They feed on ticks that live on the skin of buffaloes and other animals. If danger threatens, they fly off. Their flight helps to warn the buffaloes.

g for its life

en the four-winged flying fish is ng chased, it shoots out of the ater and glides over the top of the aves. It can stay airborne for 3,000 eet, beating the water with its tail whenever it drops down low.

On the hop

Kangaroos hop across the grassy plains of Australia at high speed. They cruise at 25 mph and reach 40 mph for short bursts, using their long tail to help them balance. One red kangaroo made a record-breaking long jump of 42 feet.

All under one roof
Social weaver birds live in Africa. In the breeding season, many pairs come together to build their nests. They build one huge domed roof of grass and straw. Then each pair builds its own nest under the roof, each with its own entrance.

Building a Castle

Many animals build homes to live in and rear their young. Some homes are small and simple, and do not last very long. Others are more like fortresses, designed to keep out unwelcome visitors and strong enough to last for years. Some animals that live in large, highly organized societies may build huge structures. Termites are particularly clever builders. Their complex homes vary to cope with different climates. In parts of Africa, the termites build a roof on their home to protect it against heavy rain. In Australia, they build tall funnels round their fortress so that hot air can escape from the nest.

Lumberjacks at work
Beavers build their home, or lodge, with wood and mud in lakes and rivers. They cut down trees by gnawing the trunks with their teeth.

First the beavers cut the trees into pieces. Then they drag or roll them into the water and build a dam to make a deep pool.

They build their lodge in the pool, using sticks and mud. It has entrances underwater, and twigs and bark are stored nearby for food.

A sticky trap
A spider's web is not its home but a food trap. Orb webs, like this one, have sticky threads that trap the spider's insect prey. Some spiders in tropical forests build huge orb webs nearly 20 feet across.

Underground town
This prairie dog is on guard duty at one of the entrances to its home, called a town. The town may contain 1,000 animals, and its burrows can stretch for miles under the ground.

Termite tower
In Australia, termites build towers 20 feet high and 100 feet wide. Ten tons of mud are collected bit by bit by millions of insects. Soldier termites guard the mud castle, where the queen lays her eggs and is fed by worker termites.

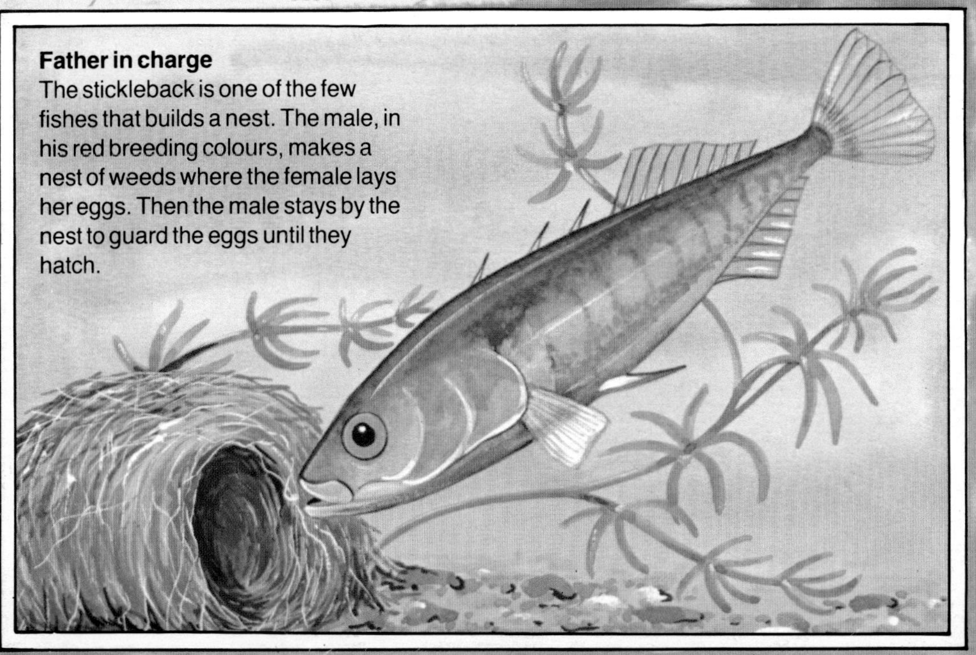

Father in charge
The stickleback is one of the few fishes that builds a nest. The male, in his red breeding colours, makes a nest of weeds where the female lays her eggs. Then the male stays by the nest to guard the eggs until they hatch.

Fantastic Feeders

Animals hunt their prey in different ways. Some hunt alone, while others find safety in numbers and hunt in groups. There are also animals that do not bother to track down their prey. Instead they wait for it to come to them, either by chance, or by luring their victim into a trap. The methods of catching and eating food are sometimes quite remarkable. In the ocean depths, anglerfish have a spine with a kind of light on the end to attract prey, while archerfish near the surface shoot jets of water at insects on the river bank. But snakes are perhaps the most extraordinary feeders of all. They can stretch their jaws so wide that even goats can be swallowed whole.

A light in the dark
It is very dark in the depths of the oceans. Deep-water anglerfish have a special way to find their prey in the dark. A long spine with a kind of light at the end lures fish into their open mouth.

A tree-climbing crab
Coconuts are plentiful on the Pacific islands where the giant robber crabs live. The crabs feed on dead animals, but they also like eating coconuts. They may carry a fallen coconut up a palm tree and then drop it to crack it open. They scoop out the flesh with a claw.

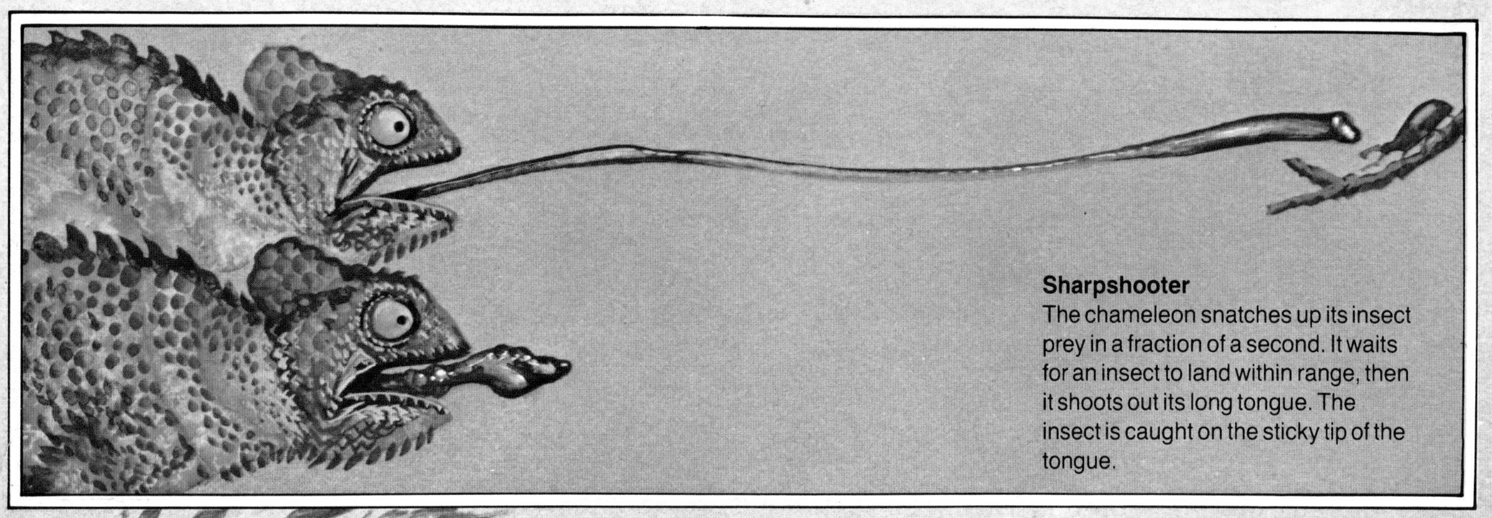

Sharpshooter
The chameleon snatches up its insect prey in a fraction of a second. It waits for an insect to land within range, then it shoots out its long tongue. The insect is caught on the sticky tip of the tongue.

Open wide
This is a rock python. Pythons and boas are large snakes that feed on animals as big as goats and deer. The snake holds its prey in its mouth, then coils itself tightly round the animal so that it cannot breathe. The snake may take several hours to swallow its meal.

Ants on the march
A column of army ants may consist of 150,000 insects and take several hours to march past one spot. They prey on almost any animal that cannot escape from them.

Deadly weapon
Swordfish use their long pointed snout to kill their prey. They rush at a shoal of smaller fish at high speed, swiping the fish with their sword to stun them. If they feel threatened by another fish, they use their sword to ram it.

Valuable fur
Today only a few hundred snow leopards are left because human hunters have killed them all for their beautiful fur. Snow leopards live in the Himalayas, where they are now a protected species.

Homeless
The Japanese crested ibis is almost extinct, although large numbers used to live in Russia, China and Japan. They nest and feed in wet, wooded areas. As more and more land has been drained and forests cleared, the birds' natural habitat has disappeared. Today only a handful of crested ibises are left. They live on a tiny Japanese island.

On the edge of extinction
The Sumatran rhinoceros is smaller than other rhinos and has two horns, not one. Only about 150 remain, but even these are in serious danger from hunters.

Mysterious decline
The rusty numbat is a rare Australian mammal. Its other name is banded anteater, although its favourite food is termites. At night, it shelters in a hollow log. It is not clear why these animals are dying out. Perhaps they are eaten by foxes, or perhaps they die in bush fires.

A Rare Sight

These are just a few of the world's rare animals. Every week, somewhere in the world, one kind of animal becomes extinct. Other animals are so rare that only one or two are still alive. There are many reasons why the numbers of certain animals are falling. Very often it is people who are responsible. We hunt animals for sport, money and food. In many parts of the world the animals' natural habitats are destroyed when land is cleared for building and farming. Waste material from factories can pollute their habitats, and destroy the food they live on. Some rare animals are now protected in special reserves and parks, but many others are still in great danger.

Mountain giant
The giant panda lives only in the bamboo forests in a remote, mountainous corner of China. It spends most of the day on the ground, feeding on bamboo, but it can climb trees. In winter it shelters from the snow in caves and hollow trees.

A tasty dish
The crested porcupine, which lives in Africa and parts of Europe, has often been hunted for its tasty meat. Now it is becoming rare.
When the porcupine meets an enemy it turns its back towards its foe and rattles its long black and white spines.

Winning the Race

Some of these animals can run much faster than the speed limit for cars on many roads. One reason they may need to run fast is to escape from their enemies. Running is the main defence of the pronghorn antelope against wolves,coyotes and even pumas. The leatherback turtle uses its speed to shake off killer whales and sharks. Other animals use their speed to catch their prey. The cheetah sprints afterThomson's gazelles, whose only hope of escape is to keep running for longer than the cheetah. The fastest bird, the spine-tailed swift, is only outpaced by birds of prey diving to snatch their victim.

Top sprinter
The cheetah races across the grassy plains of Africa at 60 mph, maybe more, arching and stretching its body to run faster. It is the fastest runner in the world, but it can only stay at top speed for a few hundred yards.

Like a torpedo
The sailfish is probably the fastest fish. To reach its top speed of 70 mph it folds its fins, even the big one, into grooves on its body so that it is more streamlined.

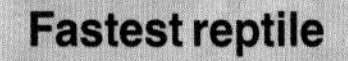

Fastest reptile
Turtles move very slowly on land, but in the water the Pacific leatherback turtle is the fastest reptile of all. It is more streamlined than other turtles and can swim at 22 mph.

Long-distance runner
The African ostrich makes up for not being able to fly by running faster than any other bird. Its strong thighs and long legs enable it to run at 30 mph for as long as half an hour, and it can reach 45 mph for a short burst.

Designed for speed
Pronghorn antelopes live on the open plains of the western United States. Their lungs and heart are large which enables them to run at a fast, steady speed for long distances. They can keep going at 35 mph for 4 miles.

Air speed record
Swifts fly faster and spend more time in the air than any other bird. They are easily recognized by their long curved wings. The fastest of all is the spine-tailed swift, which lives in Asia and can fly at 100 mph. Like other swifts it spends at least 9 months of the year on the wing, feeding, resting and even mating in the air. It only lands in the breeding season, when it builds a nest of moss and hairs in tree holes.

Speedy insect
The day-flying hummingbird hawkmoth relies on speed to avoid capture. Hawkmoths are among the swiftest flying insects, reaching 30 mph.

Darting flight
Dragonflies are also fast-flying insects, especially the darter dragonflies which are named after the way they dart about.

On the Move

All kinds of tags, rings and even tiny radio transmitters are fixed on to animals to find out about their movements round the world. The distances covered may be quite spectacular. Even fragile insects like butterflies can travel more than 4,000 miles in a lifetime. Some animals migrate between their warm winter quarters and their breeding grounds. Others make long journeys to find food. Migratory animals have remarkable powers of navigation. Birds use the sun as a kind of compass or navigate by the stars. And when salmon move upstream to spawn they use their sense of smell to find their way to the spot where they themselves hatched.

Butterfly trees
Some monarch butterflies fly from Canada to Mexico, where they mass together on trees to hibernate for the winter.

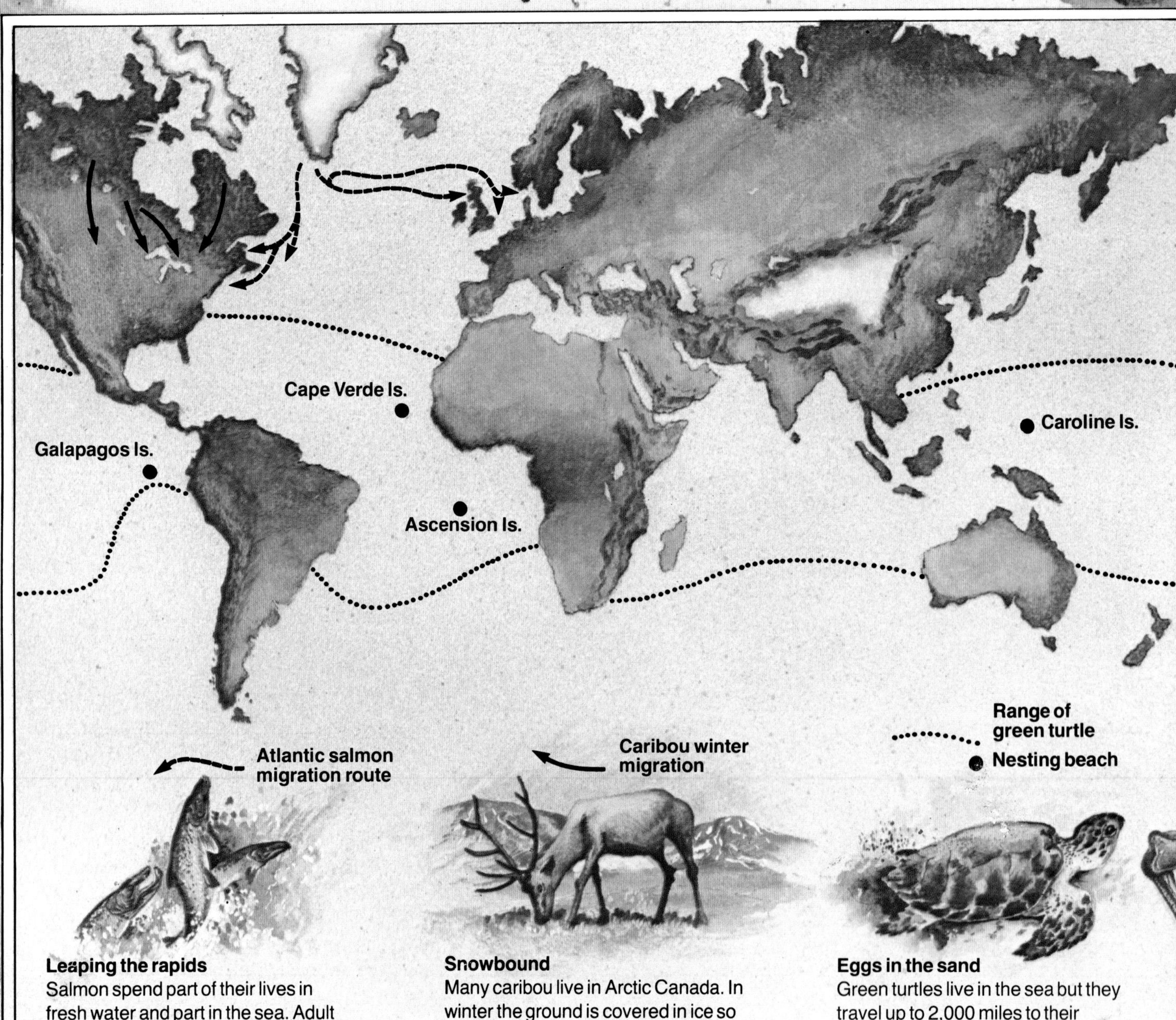

Leaping the rapids
Salmon spend part of their lives in fresh water and part in the sea. Adult salmon leave the sea and move up-river, often leaping rapids on the way, to lay their eggs.

Snowbound
Many caribou live in Arctic Canada. In winter the ground is covered in ice so the caribou move south in search of moss and lichen to feed on. They return to the north in the spring.

Eggs in the sand
Green turtles live in the sea but they travel up to 2,000 miles to their island breeding grounds. The females crawl up the beach and lay their eggs in a pit in the sand.

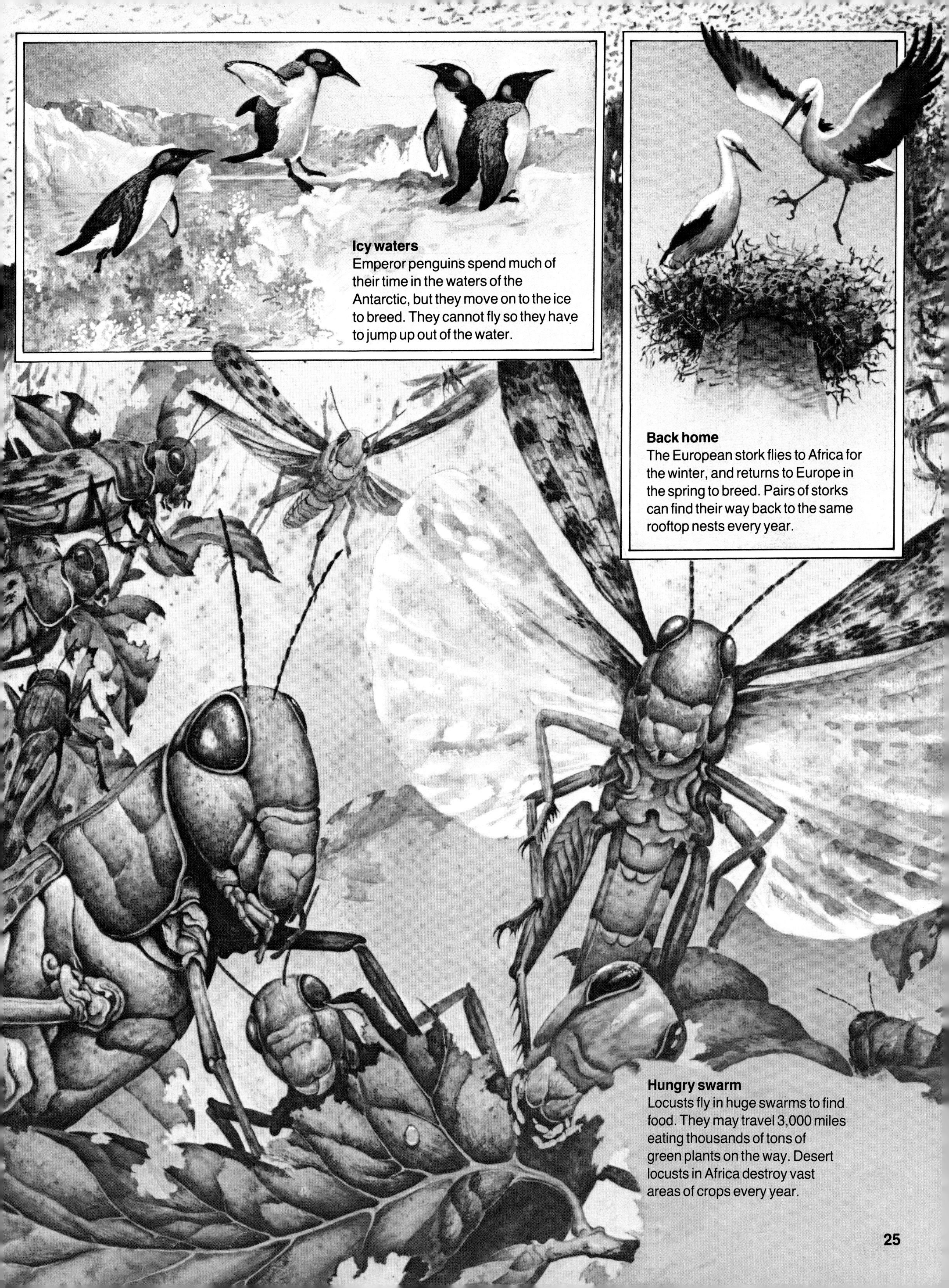

Icy waters
Emperor penguins spend much of their time in the waters of the Antarctic, but they move on to the ice to breed. They cannot fly so they have to jump up out of the water.

Back home
The European stork flies to Africa for the winter, and returns to Europe in the spring to breed. Pairs of storks can find their way back to the same rooftop nests every year.

Hungry swarm
Locusts fly in huge swarms to find food. They may travel 3,000 miles eating thousands of tons of green plants on the way. Desert locusts in Africa destroy vast areas of crops every year.

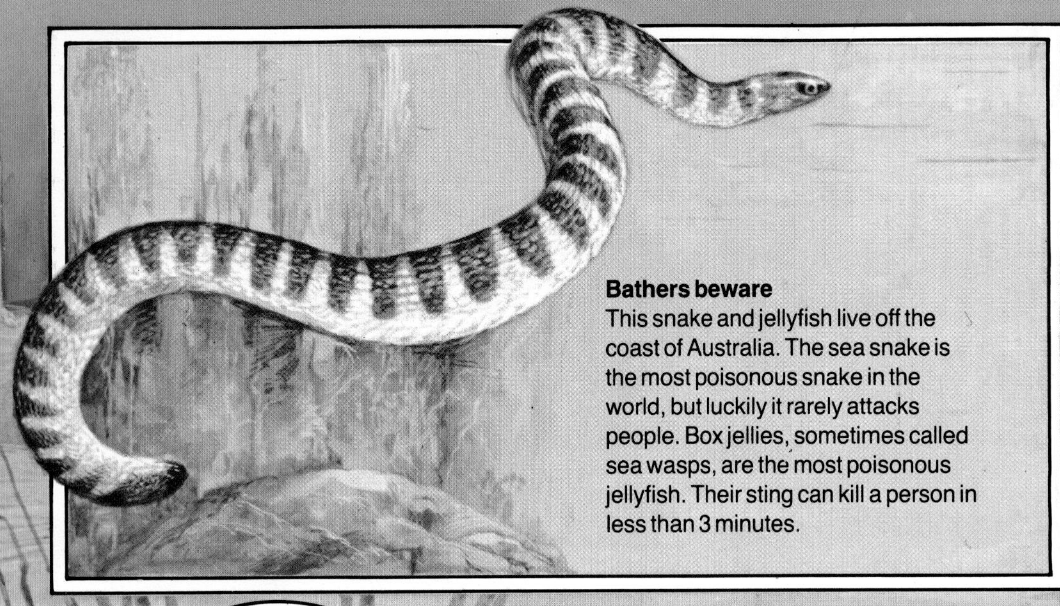

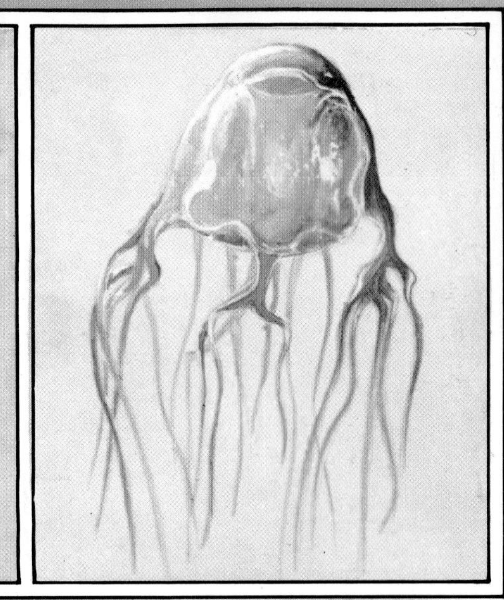

Bathers beware
This snake and jellyfish live off the coast of Australia. The sea snake is the most poisonous snake in the world, but luckily it rarely attacks people. Box jellies, sometimes called sea wasps, are the most poisonous jellyfish. Their sting can kill a person in less than 3 minutes.

Poisoned arrows
Some South American frogs have poison in their skin, although the poison is not always deadly. They are known as arrow-poison frogs because Indian hunters use the poison to tip their arrows.

Fatal sting
Scorpions use their poison for attack and defence. Some kinds of scorpion have a sting that is so powerful it can kill people.

Danger in the desert
The North American harvester ants can give people a nasty sting. They live in deserts, where they build volcano-shaped nests in the sand. The ants feed on grass seeds.

Deadly Poison

Animals that produce poison use it as a weapon against their enemies or to attack their prey. Poison used in defence does not always kill, but simply wards off the enemy. Frogs with poisonous skins taste unpleasant, so the predator releases them. Some animals produce just enough poison to stun their enemy long enough for them to escape. One snake, the black-necked cobra, can spit venom as far as 8 feet. The most poisonous animals are not always the most dangerous for humans, since they often live in places where few people go. Animals that produce a less toxic venom but which live near people are more likely to attack and cause harm.

Poisonous bite
The Gila monster is one of the two poisonous lizards in the world. When it bites its prey, such as mice and rabbits, it squirts poison down through grooves in its teeth.

Two of a kind
The beaded lizard (above) and the Gila monster are the only poisonous lizards in the world. They wander over the prairies and deserts of North America.

Deadly female
The most poisonous spider of all is probably the American black widow. The female is more dangerous than the male. Its bite is extremely painful and sometimes causes death.

Death in disguise
The well-camouflaged stonefish lives in warm seas, where it lies hidden on coral reefs. If its spines are touched they give out a poison which can kill a person in a few hours.

Disappearing Tricks

Camouflage is a very common method of defence in the animal kingdom. It may also help animals who are hunting to approach their prey unseen. The colours and patterns on an animal's skin often match its surroundings perfectly, and some animals can also change colour as they move about. There are insects that imitate the foliage on which they live so precisely that they virtually disappear. If these disguises do not work, some animals may try to distract their predators. For example, when a nesting ringed plover is disturbed, it creeps away from the nest unseen, then flies noisily off. Its enemies then have no idea where the bird's eggs really are.

Pebbles on the beach
Plovers lay their eggs on sand or shingle. They do not build a nest because this would attract attention to the eggs. Very often, each egg has different markings to blend with the pebbles. When the chicks hatch, they too are well camouflaged on the seashore.

Stripes for stalking
A tiger's stripes help to break up the outline of its body and make it hard to see. They also look like shadows as the tiger stalks through long grass in the moonlight. Tigers live in Asia. Those that live in hot countries often sit in shallow water to keep cool. Tigers in very cold countries have thick shaggy coats to keep them warm.

All change
The octopus can change its colour in seconds as it moves across different backgrounds. Most can turn red, yellow and black, or mixtures of these colours. Some can even make their smooth skin bumpy.

Winter coat
Several animals that live in the far north, like this stoat, become white in the winter to blend in with the snow. They moult and grow a thicker coat. Some Arctic birds change colour, too, and grow white feathers.

Fishy disguise
The Sargassum fish (below) looks very like the seaweed that grows in the Sargasso Sea, where it lives. These long, slim pipefish (right) are cousins of the sea-horses. Their dull colour and reed-like shape disguise them among clumps of eel-grass.

Safe among the flowers
The flower mantis (left) may be pink or white, and has petal shapes on its body. With this disguise it can rest among flowers without being spotted by the birds that feed on it. The mantis eats bees, butterflies and other insects, which may be attracted by its flower shape.

Like a twig
Many caterpillars use camouflage to hide them from their enemies. The geometer moth caterpillars (right) look just like twigs, and can hold themselves at an angle from plant stems as if they were growing. They even have bumps that look like buds.

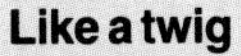

Animal Facts and Feats

Research into the behaviour and achievements of animals in the wild is not always easy. Some animals are very rare and difficult to find. Others live in remote or mountainous areas where few people see them. Zoologists may have to spend months or even years making detailed observations of an animal before its habits are properly understood. A certain amount can be learned from animals in captivity. For example, most of the figures given below for the longest-lived animals were recorded in zoos where accurate records of ages can be kept.

Mammals

Largest and heaviest
Blue whale
Average length 100 ft
Largest ever recorded 110 ft
Pregnant female may weight 200 tons

Smallest land mammal
Kitti's hog-nosed bat (Thailand)
Wing span 6 ins
Weight .05 to .07 oz

Smallest marine animal
Probably Heaviside's dolphin (South Atlantic)
Length 4 ft
Weight 9 lbs

Rarest
A species of tenrec from Madagascar is only known from a single specimen.

Fastest
Cheetah (Africa, Middle East, W. Asia)
Can run at 60 mph over short distances.
Pronghorn antelope (USA)
Can run at 40 mph over long distances.

Slowest
Three-toed sloth (South America)
Covers about 15 ft a minute in trees, and only 6 ft a minute on the ground.

Highest
Yak (China and Tibet)
Climbs to 20,000 ft to feed.

Reptiles

Largest and heaviest
Estuarine crocodile (Asia, Australia)
Average length, male up to 14 ft
Longest ever recorded 27 ft

Fastest
(on land) Six-lined racerunner (USA)
Can run at 18 mph
(in water) Pacific leatherback turtle
Can swim at 22 mph

Largest lizard
Komodo dragon (Indonesian islands)
Length up to 10 ft

Largest turtle
Pacific leatherback turtle
Average length, male up to 7 ft
Weight up to 800 lbs

Longest snake
Reticulated python (India and S.E. Asia)
Average length more than 20 ft
Longest ever recorded 32 ft 9½ ins

Most poisonous snake
Sea snake (off N.W. Australia)

Most poisonous land snake
Fierce snake (Australia) has most toxic venom.

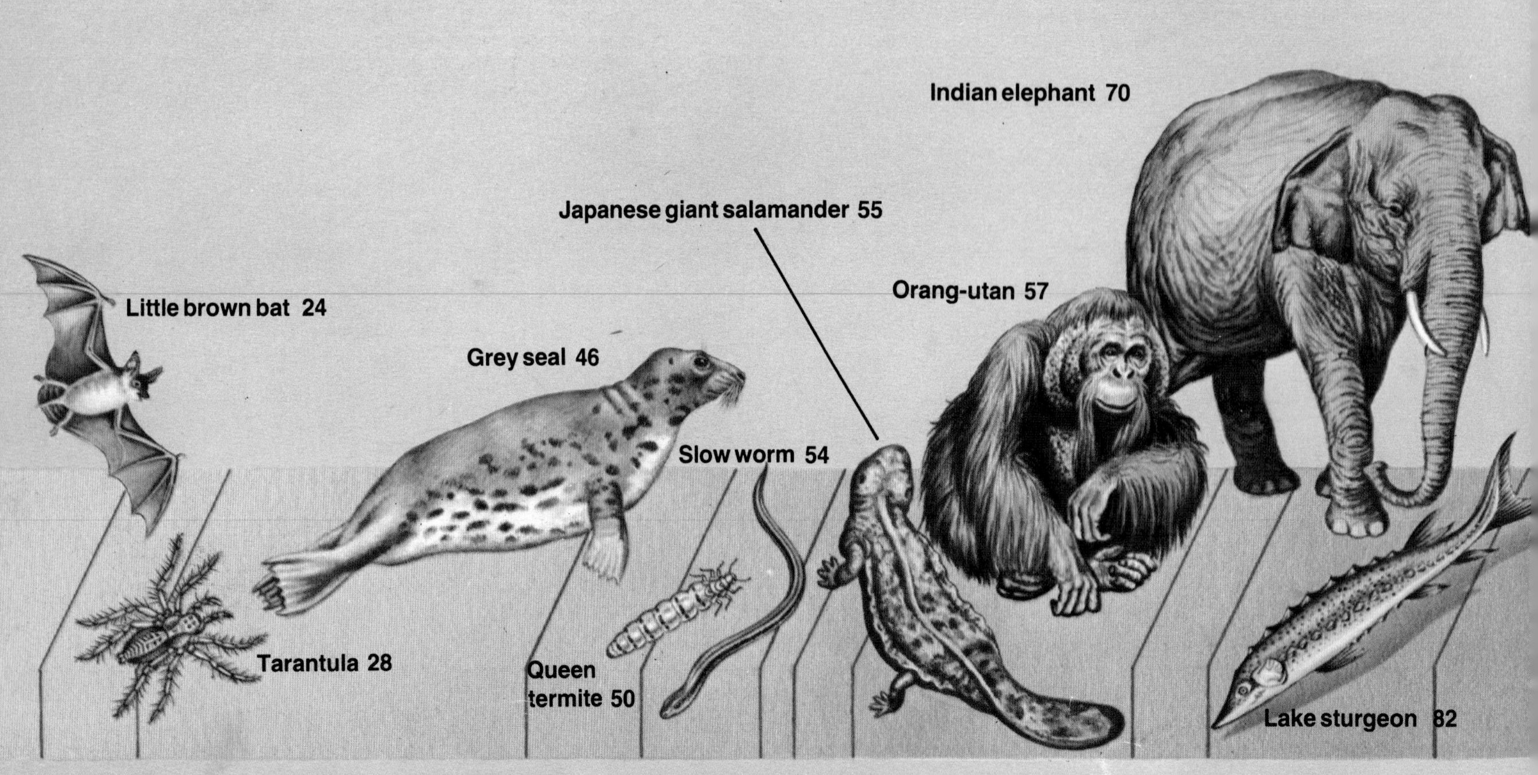

Amphibians

Largest
Chinese giant salamander
Average length 3 ft
Longest ever recorded 5 ft
Weight 24-28 lbs
Highest
Common toad
One found at 26,000 ft in Himalayas
Most poisonous
Kokoi arrow-poison frog (South America)
A tiny amount of toxin is enough to kill a man.
Largest newt
Ribbed newt (Africa)
Length up to 15 ins
Weight 1 lb
Smallest newt
Striped newt (USA)
Length 2 ins
Largest frog
Goliath frog (Africa)
Length of body 13 ins
Largest toad
Probably marine toad (South America)
Length 9 ins

Longest lived
Few animals live longer than human beings. Tortoises have the greatest life-span of all the backboned animals. Many different species are known to live for over 100 years. Some of the ages given below were recorded in zoo specimens.

Ages in years

Birds

Largest (but flightless)
North African ostrich
Height, male 9 ft
Weight 345 lbs
Egg up to 8 ins long
Largest wing span
Wandering albatross (southern oceans)
Average wing span, male 10 ft
Largest ever recorded 11 ft 10 ins
Smallest
Helena's hummingbird (Cuba)
Average length, male 2¼ ins (head and body ½ in)
Weight .07 oz
Egg .45 ins long
Rarest (bird of prey)
Mauritius kestrel (Mauritius)
About 5 are thought to remain
Fastest
Spine-tailed swift (Russia and Himalayas)
Flies at 110 mph
Longest flight
Arctic tern
May cover 25,000 miles a year migrating from Arctic to Antarctic and back.
Fastest under water
Gentoo penguin
Swims at 22 mph
Largest nest
Bald eagles
One was 9½ ft wide and 20 ft deep

Fishes

Largest (plankton-eating)
Whale shark
Largest ever recorded 59 ft long
Largest (meat-eating)
Great white shark (the 'man-eater')
Average length up to 15 ft
Longest bony fish
Russian sturgeon (or Beluga)
Length up to 26 ft 3 ins
Heaviest bony fish
Ocean sunfish
Largest ever recorded 2.24 tons
Fastest
Probably sailfish
Fastest ever recorded 68.1 mph
Most poisonous
Stonefish (Indian and Pacific Oceans)
Poison carried in spines can cause a person's death within a few hours.
Most electric
Electric eel (South America)
Can produce 400 to 650 volts.

Insects

Heaviest
Goliath beetle (Africa)
Weight, male 3.52 oz
Longest
A tropical stick insect
Length up to 13 ins
Largest butterfly
Queen Alexandra birdwing (New Guinea)
Wing span 12 ins
Weight 0.176 oz
Most dangerous ant
Black bulldog ant (Australia and Tasmania)
One bite can kill a man.
Fastest wing beat
A tiny midge can beat its wings 1,000 times a second.
Largest locust swarm
A swarm of desert locusts that crossed the Red Sea in 1889. Swarm estimated to contain 250,000,000 insects, weighing about 500,000 tons and covering 2,000 square miles.

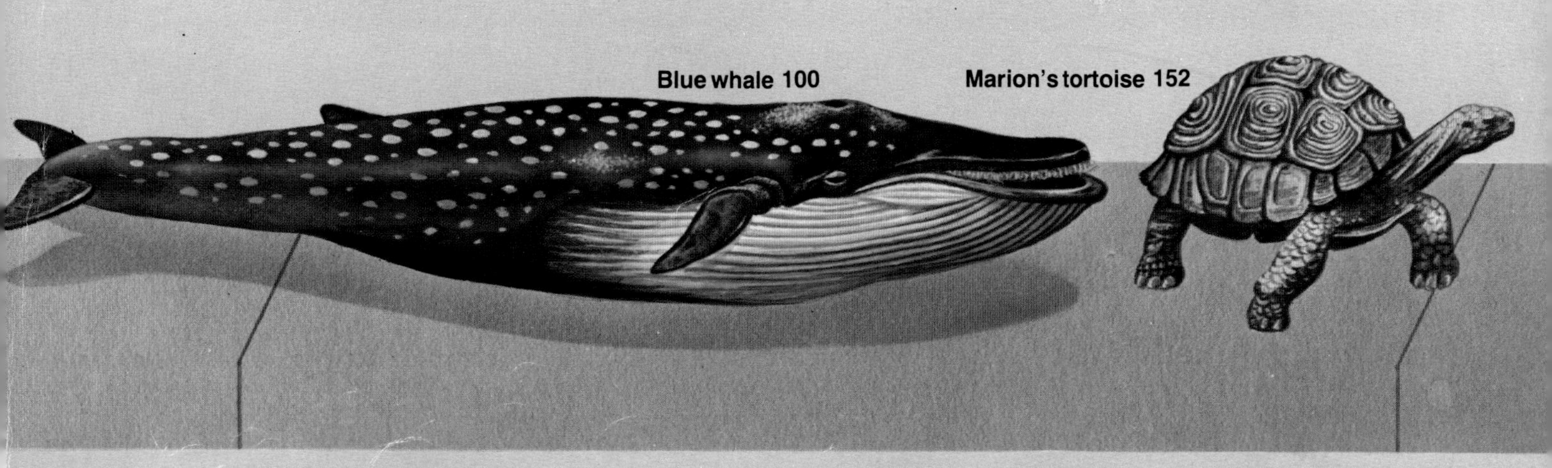

Index

We are very grateful to Guinness Superlatives Ltd. for their kind permission to make use of certain facts and figures from the Guinness Book of Records (1980 edition) in the compilation of this book.